MW01609868

Encyclopedia of

CAT JOKES

If You Ever Had a Cat, You NEED This Book.

Cat jokes do *not* have to be stupid.
This book has some of the funniest
cat jokes ever thunk up, and stolen.
(I mean, *borrowed*).

Compiled by Nick Hetcher
The Godfather of Cat Jokes

ISBN: 9798850410438

Reasons YOU Should Laugh More

Cats flat out ROCK!! I love them!! Our two *(Charlie and Chelsie)* are the best!! They make us laugh and entertain us all day, every day. I'll bet your cats are the delight of your home, too.

My mission for this book is to bring more laughter into this crazy world we live in. It doesn't matter who we are, a little laughter each day can go a long way.

Laughter has been proven medically to relieve stress, a major cause of many of today's diseases. Laughter has been medically proven to: boost immunity, improve heart health, clear the mind, kill pain *(it releases endorphins)*, relax your body, stir up creativity, burn calories, lower blood pressure, fight depression, improve memory, improve blood flow, improve memory (lol), and reduce inflammation. Laughter helps to build great friendships.

It's great in marriage *(unless your wife starts telling her friends that YOU are a joke).* Laughter breaks a somber mood. Laughter is magical.

The Bible sums it up… "Laughter is good medicine." Proverbs 17:22. I hope this book makes you laugh a little bit more each day, and even causes you to spread that cheer to the world around you.

Frankly, I got tired of the stale, wornout, *somewhat* funny cat jokes going around, just making cat's look stupid. Not much better than dogs. How sad. Am I right or am I right? So, I decided it's due time to step it up with actually hilarious kitty jokes.

Oh, and of course I can't forget to say… this book makes a great gift so make sure to have several copies on hand to give to the cat lovers *(and haters)* in your life. Even dog lovers just to annoy them. Order several copies now, I need a vacation. :-)

All kidding aside *(for the moment anyway)*... I really do hope you enjoy this book. I personally handpicked every joke for my laughing pleasure. I mean, yours. Much love and lots of laughs in your life. God Bless you and our wonderful cats.

- Nick Hetcher
Self proclaimed "Godfather of Cat Jokes"

CAT JOKES

My wife wanted me to buy her a Siamese cat but they're really expensive. So I stole 2 normal cats and glued their heads together.

Don't order Siamese cats on the Internet. They only send you one cat, and it doesn't even have two heads.

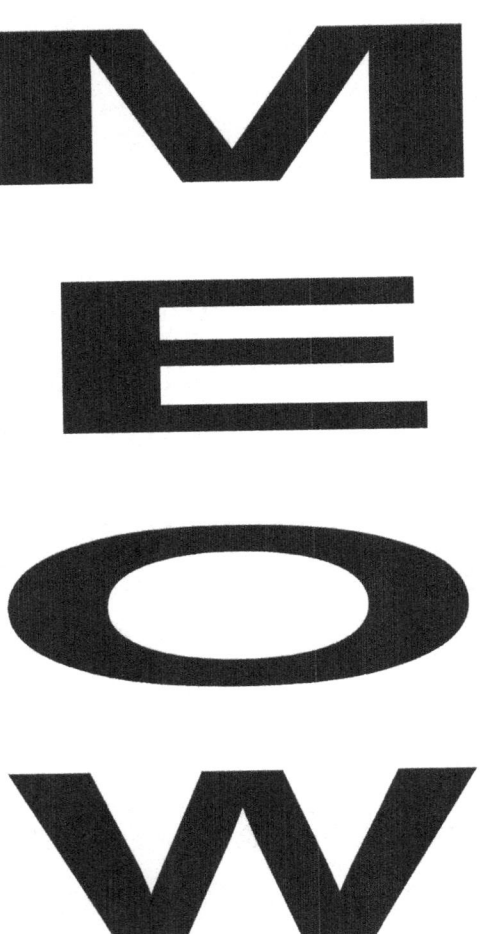

To a Cat, people are just furniture that does tricks.

My cat is so ugly when we tried to enter an ugly cat contest they said, "Sorry, no professionals."

I wrote a book on cats. I should have used paper. Yesterday, Chapter Six got hit by a car.

My cat is so ugly we have to feed him with a slingshot.

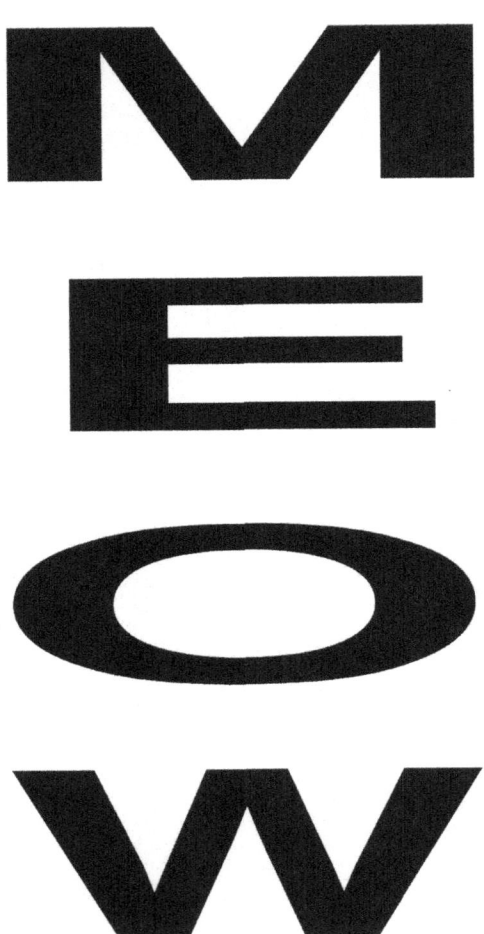

What sport do cats play? Hairball!

Why isn't there *mouse* flavored cat food?

My cat Charlie... "Please God, if you can't make me thin, make all my friends fat like Garfield."

How do cats stop crimes? They call *claw enforcement.*

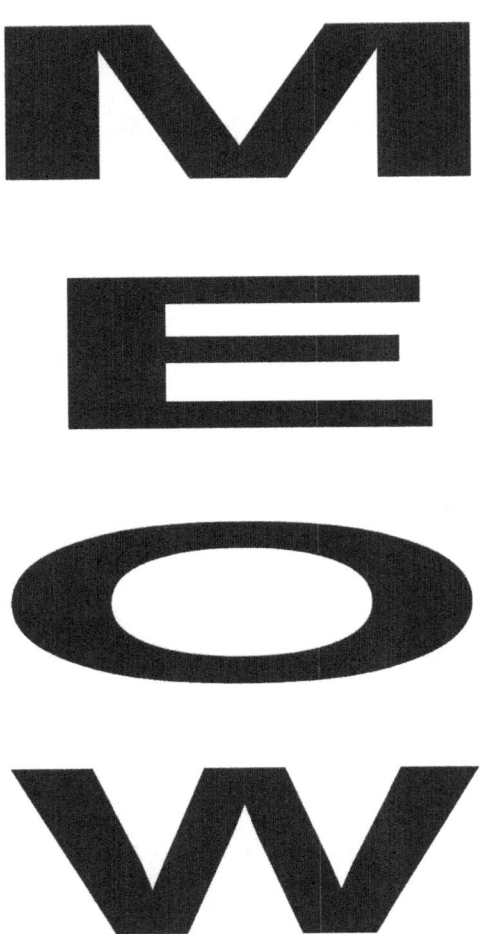

My cat is so ugly she made my *Happy Meal* cry.

My cat is so stupid, he put two quarters in his ears and thought he was listening to 50 Cent.

My cat is so ugly he has to sneak up on the mirror.

My cat is so ugly when the devil saw her, he started praying.

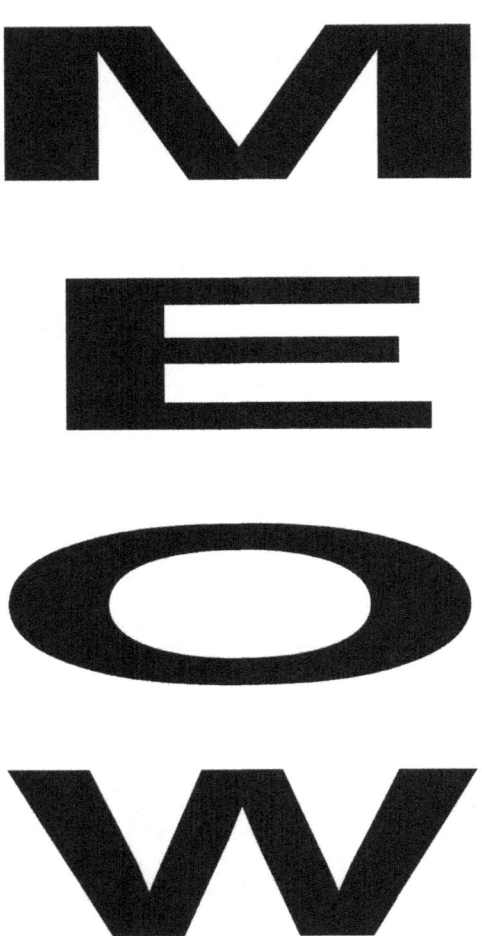

My cat is so stupid he climbed over a glass wall to see what was on the other side.

My cat is so ugly he made an onion cry.

My cat is so dumb she thought *Dunkin' Donuts* was a basketball team.

My cat is so ugly even *HelloKitty* said, "Goodbye" to him.

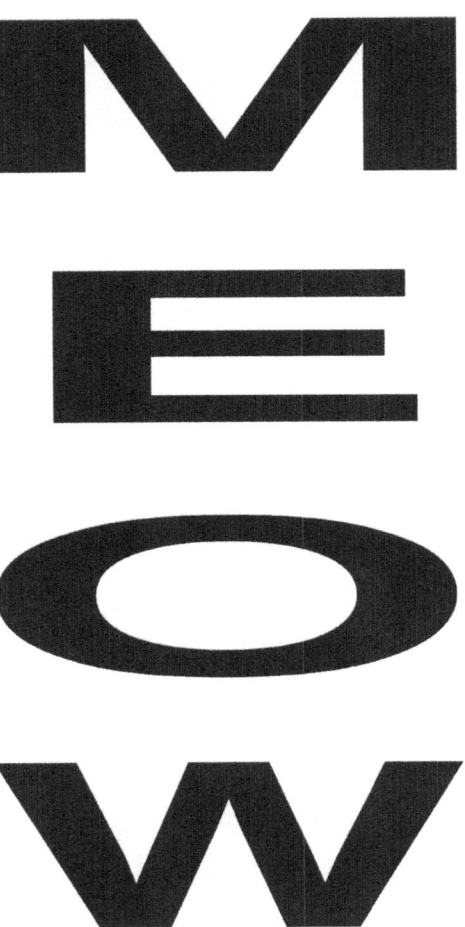

My cat is so dumb when she was locked in a grocery store she starved to death!

My cat is so ugly when she went into a haunted house, she came out with a job application.

Why are kittens actually excellent bosses? They have great littership.

My cat is so old, her birth certificate says "expired" on it.

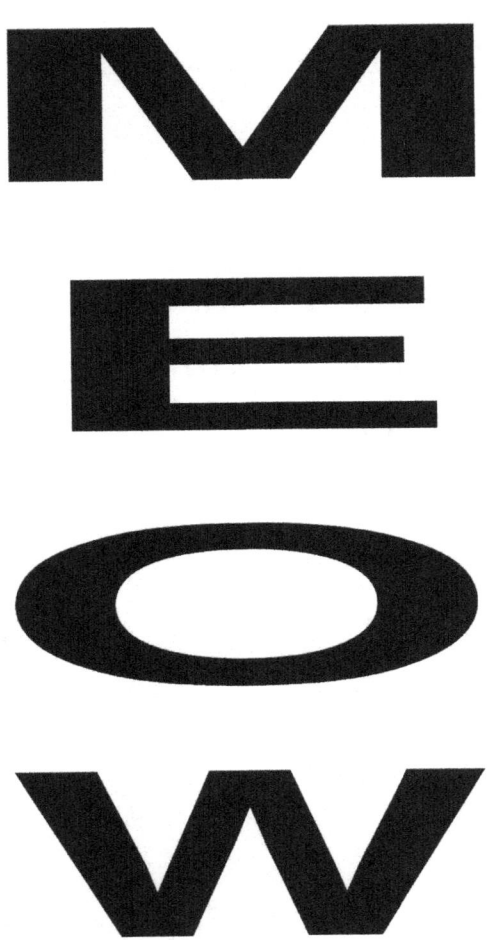

What's black and has four legs? My Siamese after I tried to light one of her farts.

My cat's teeth are so yellow, that when he smiles, traffic slows down.

Facebook is a lot like ancient Egypt. People writing on walls and worshipping cats.

My cat is so ugly she gives *Freddy Krueger* nightmares.

MEOW

My cat is so stupid, he tries to save fish from drowning.

My cat is so ugly, the government moved Halloween to her birthday!

What's black, white and red all over? Half a cat.

What do you get if you cross a cat with *Father Christmas*? Santa Claws!

MEOW

Did you know the word ho**meow**ner, has the word "meow" in it? Good luck pronouncing it correctly ever again.

What does a cat have that no other animal has? Kittens.

What's a cat's favorite magazine? *Good Mousekeeping*!

What would a cat say if you stepped on its tail? "Me-OW!"

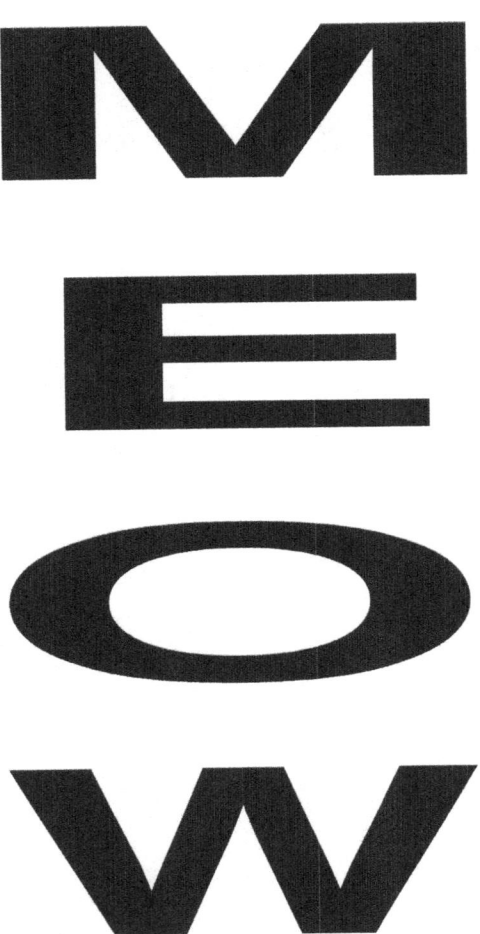

Why did the cat sleep under the car? Because she wanted to wake up oily!

My cat is so old, when she was young, rainbows were still black and white.

In what kind of weather is a vet the busiest? When it's raining cats and dogs. *(Boo)*

What do cats like to eat on a hot day? A mice-cream cone!

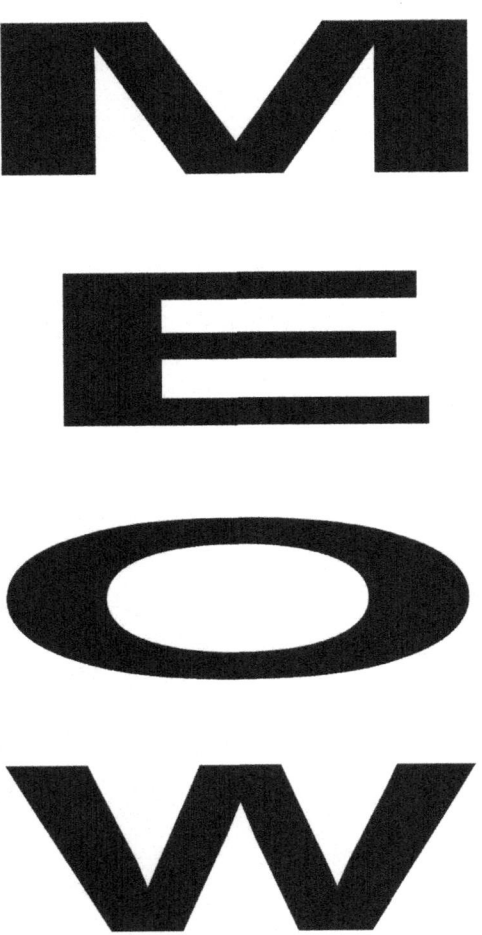

My cat is really smart. I asked him, "what's seven minus seven?" He said nothing.

How do two cats end a fight? They hiss and make up!

What's a cat's favorite TV show? *Claw and Order*.

Why do cats always get their way? They are very purr-suasive!

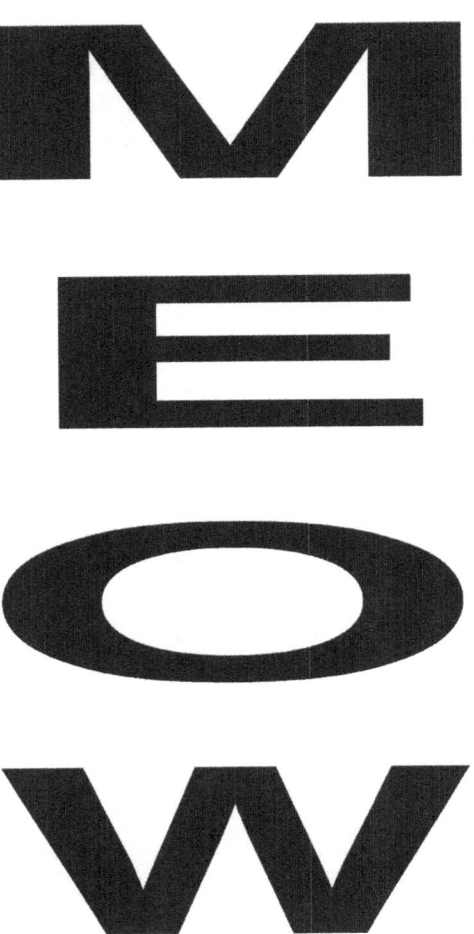

What's a cat's favorite subject in school? Hisss-tory!

The hardest part of owning a cat is telling him he's adopted.

Why did the cat have to go to an accountant? He got caught up in a purramid scheme.

Hey Alexa, clean the cat little box.

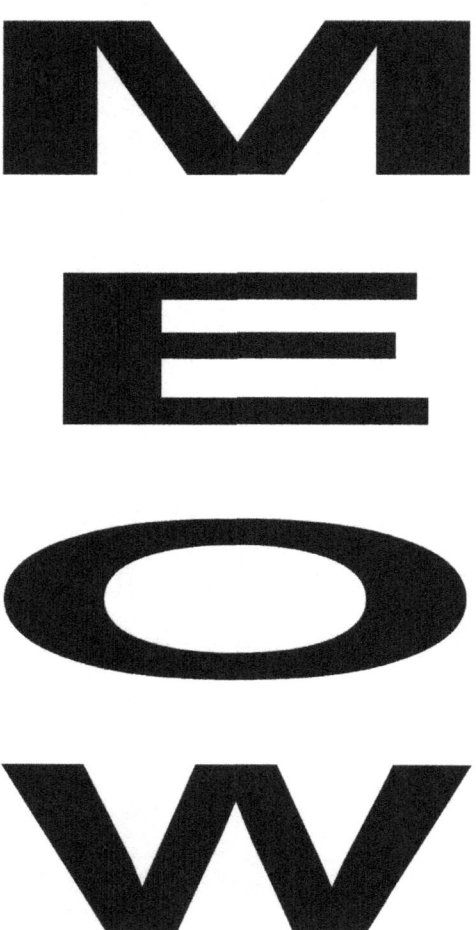

Why don't cats play poker in the wild? Too many Cheetahs!

Before going after a mouse, what did the dad cat say to his family? "Let us prey."

What do you call a cat who likes to bowl? An alley cat!

Why was the cat sitting on the computer? It wanted to keep an eye on the mouse!

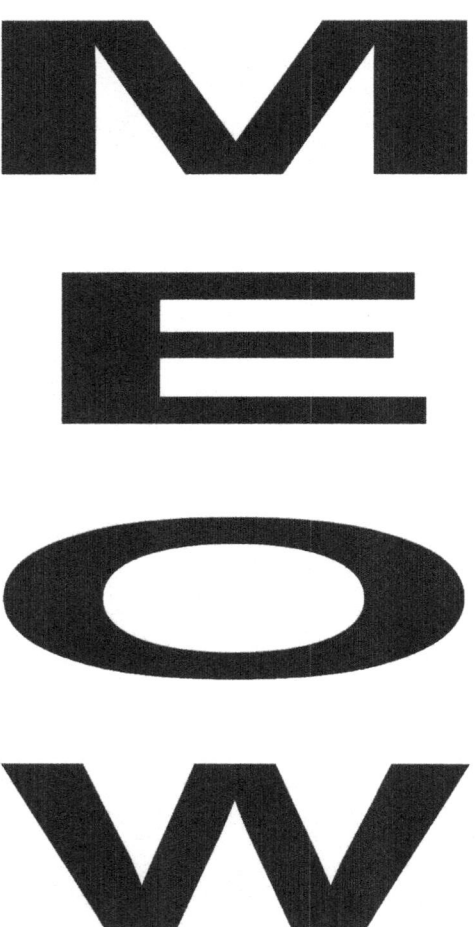

What do you call a cat that gets everything it wants? Purrr-suasive!

Why did the cat join the Red Cross? It wanted to be a first-aid purr-ovider!

What's a cat's favorite movie? The Purrsuit of Happiness!

What do you get if you cross a cat with a parrot? A carrot!

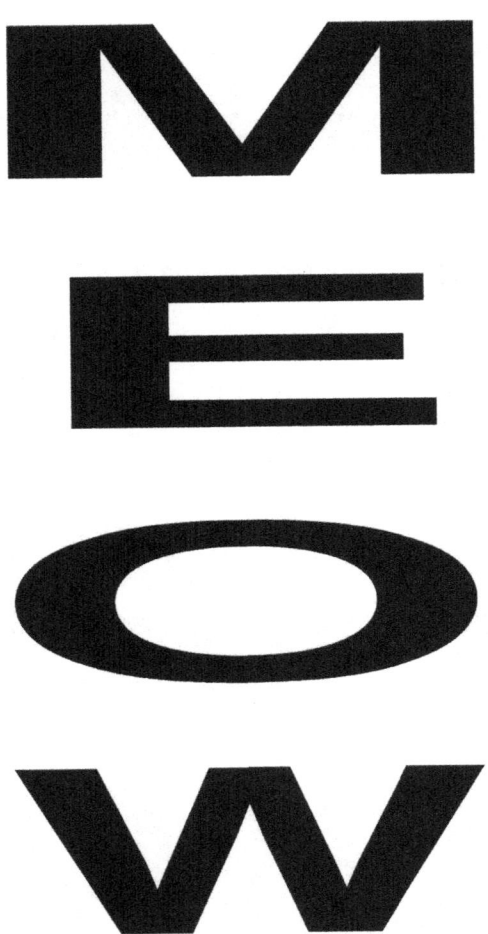

What do you call a cat that gets caught by the police? The purr-petrator!

What do you call a cat that can sing? *Kitty Perry!*

Why did the cat go to medical school? To become a purr-diatrician!

When a cat doesn't want to say goodbye, what do they say instead? "See ya litter!"

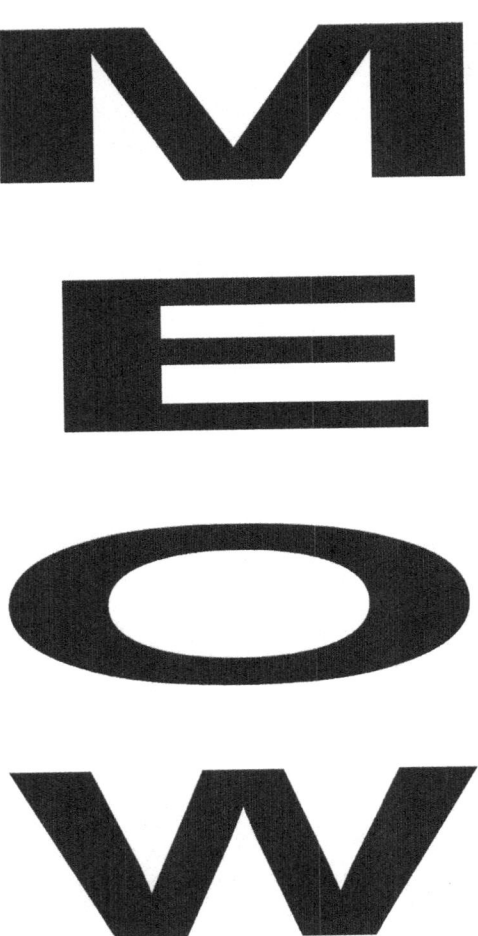

What do you call a cat that can bounce? A purr-ball!

Why did the cat go to the beauty salon? It needed a new purr-spective!

What do you call a cat that can fly? *Kitty-hawk!*

Why did the cat bring a ladder to the bar? It heard the drinks were on the house!

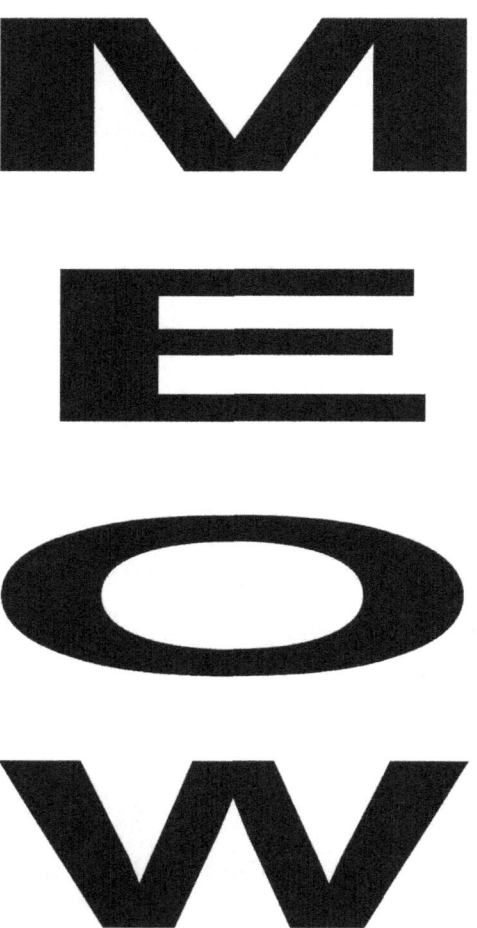

How do you know when a cat has been using your computer? The mouse pad has claw marks!

What's a cat's favorite type of clothing? Purr-jamas!

What's a cat's favorite drink? Mice tea!

What do you call a cat that likes to dig in the garden? A flower purr-son!

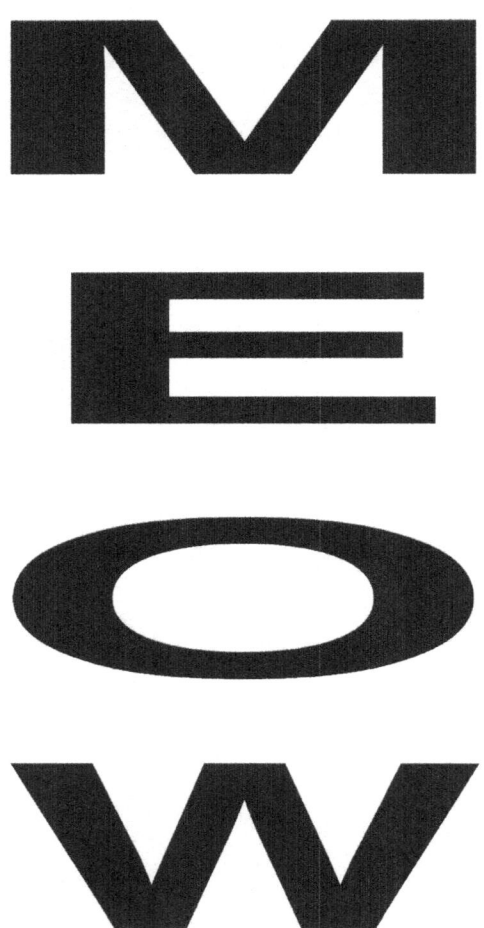

Why did the cat go to therapy?
It had too many purr-sonality
issues!

What do you call a cat that can
bark? A dog in disguise!

What do you call a cat that
likes to swim? A catfish!

Why did the cat avoid eating
lemons? They made him a
sour-puss.

What do you call a cat that can drive a race car? A furr-ari driver!

Why did the cat go to school? To improve its purr-formance!

What do you call a cat that can do tricks? A purr-former!

What do you call a cat that likes to sing? *Meow-ton John!*

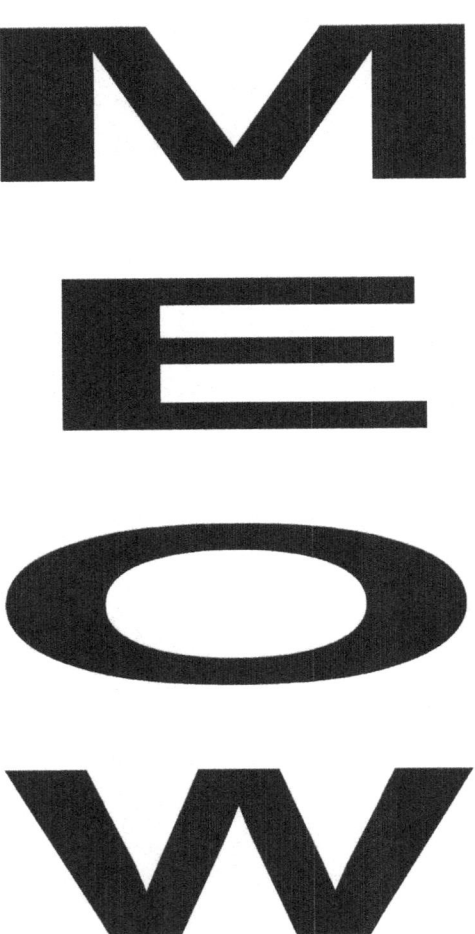

What did the cat say to the dog? "You've cat to be kitten me right meow!"

How do cats bake cakes? They use purr-servatives!

What do you call a cat that can solve math problems? A calcu-litter!

How does a cat ask for food politely? It says, "Purr-lease!"

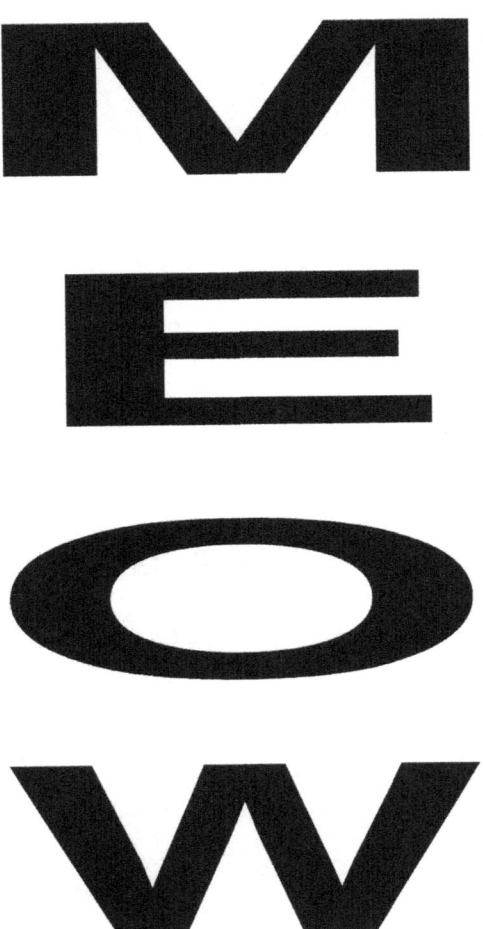

Why did the cat go to the movie theater? It heard they were playing a claw-sic!

What is the cat's favorite instrument? Purr-cussion!

What's a cat's favorite magazine? Good Mousekeeping.

What do you call it when a cat has a temper tantrum? A hissy fit.

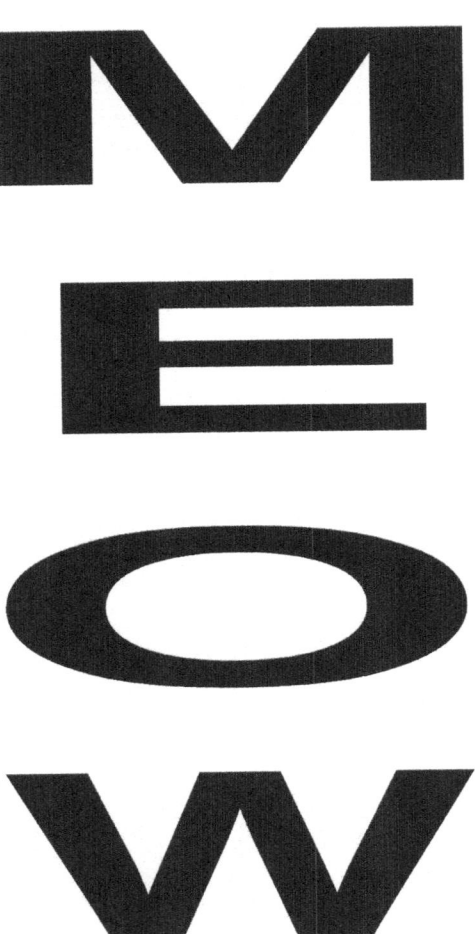

FAT CAT JOKES

To share with all your cat friends!!

My cat is so fat, that when he went to the zoo, the hippos got jealous.

My cat is so fat, when she gets in an elevator, it *has* to go down.

What's a fat cat's favorite exercise? Paw-lates.

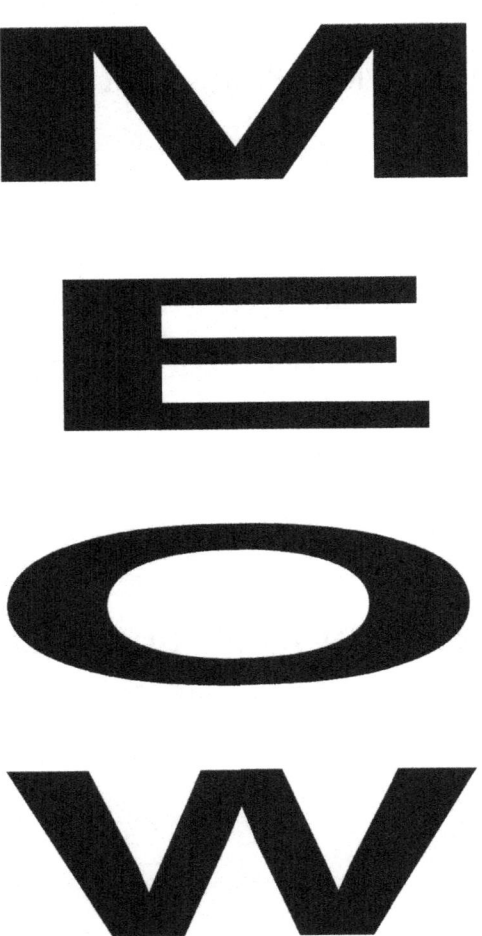

My cat is so fat she uses the interstate as a slip-and-slide.

My cat is so fat when he got on the scale it said, "I need your weight, not your phone number."

My cat is so fat and old when God said, "Let there be light," he asked my cat to move out of the way.

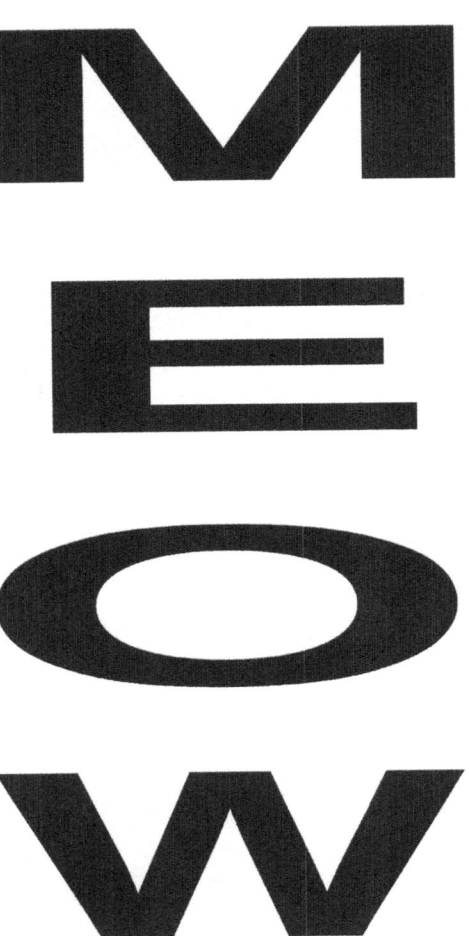

My cat is so fat, I took a picture of her during the pandemic and it's still printing.

My cat is so fat, when he farted this morning, he launched himself into orbit.

My cat is so fat she has her own zip code.

My cat is so fat that Dora can't even explore him.

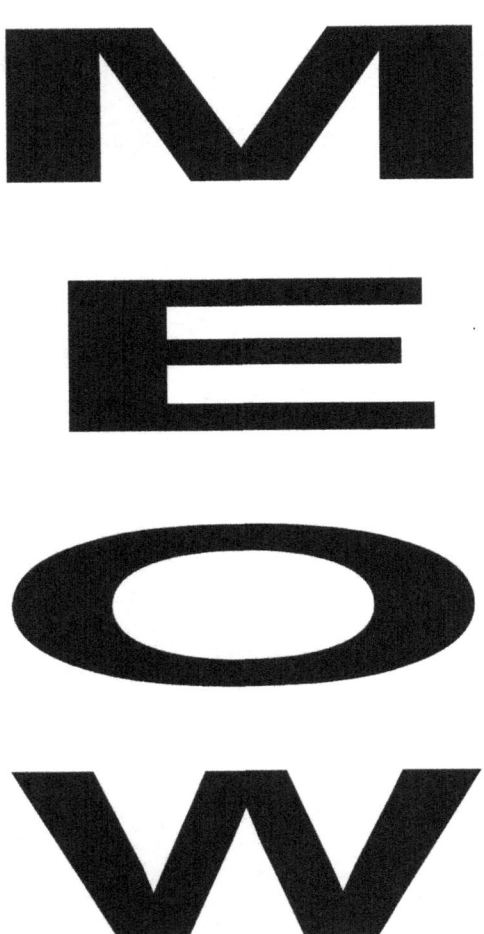

My cat is so fat, that when she fell, no one was laughing, but the ground was cracking up.

My cat is so fat and ugly, he even scares blind kids.

My cat is so fat, when she went to KFC with me, the cashier asked, "What size bucket?" and she said, "The one on your roof."

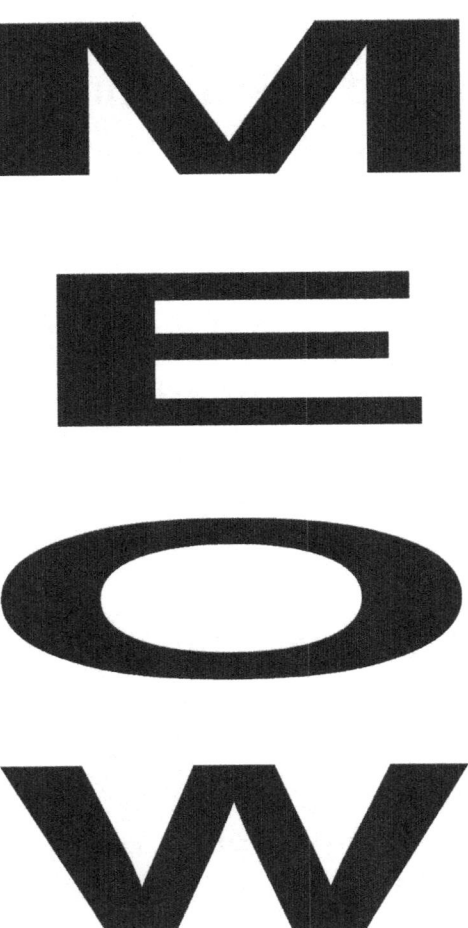

My cat is so fat, when she sat on the back of the bus it did a wheelie.

My cat is so fat he walked past the TV, and I missed 3 shows.

My cat is so fat, she has more rolls than a bakery.

My cat is so fat that when he saw a yellow school bus go by full of white kids, he ran after it yelling, "TWINKIE!"

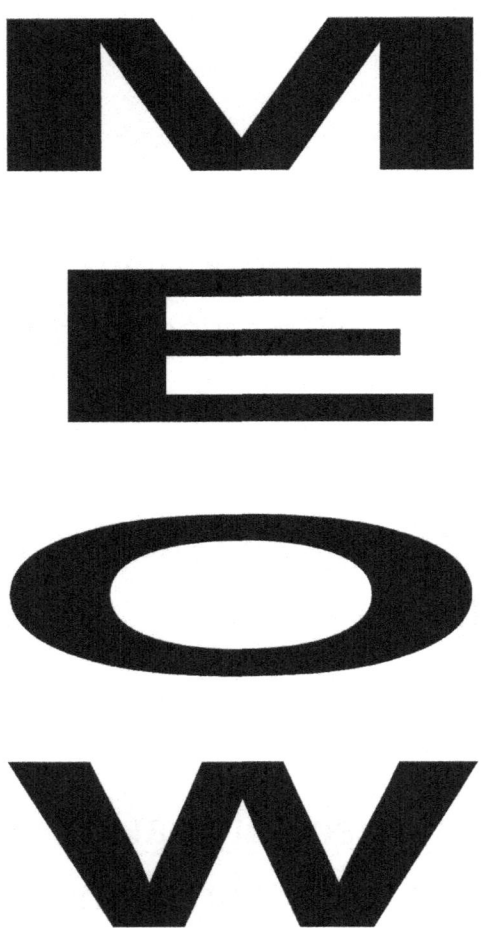

My cat is so fat, she got baptized at Sea World.

My cat is so fat I tried driving around him and I ran out of gas.

My cat is so fat, her baby pictures were taken by satellite.

My cat is so fat she can't even jump to a conclusion.

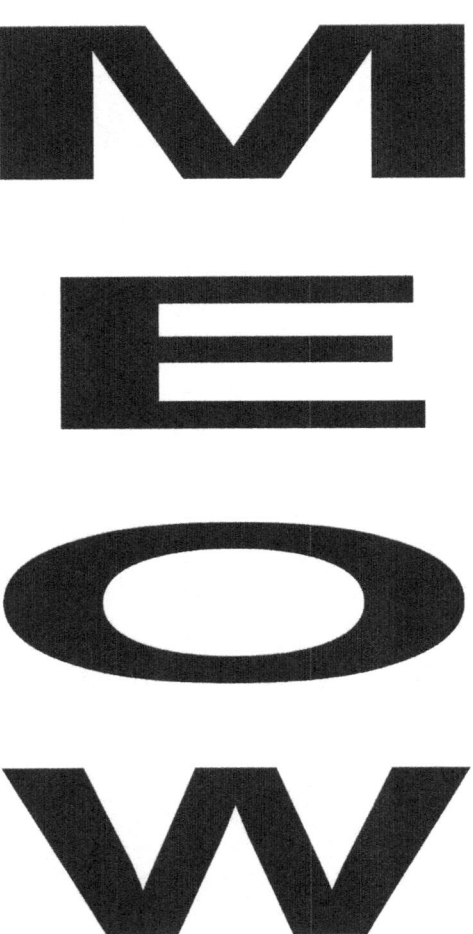

My cat is so fat, when he stepped on a scale it said, "Only one cat at a time please."

My cat is so fat when she died she broke the *Stairway to Heaven.*

My cat is so fat on Halloween he threw on a white sheet and went as *Antarctica.*

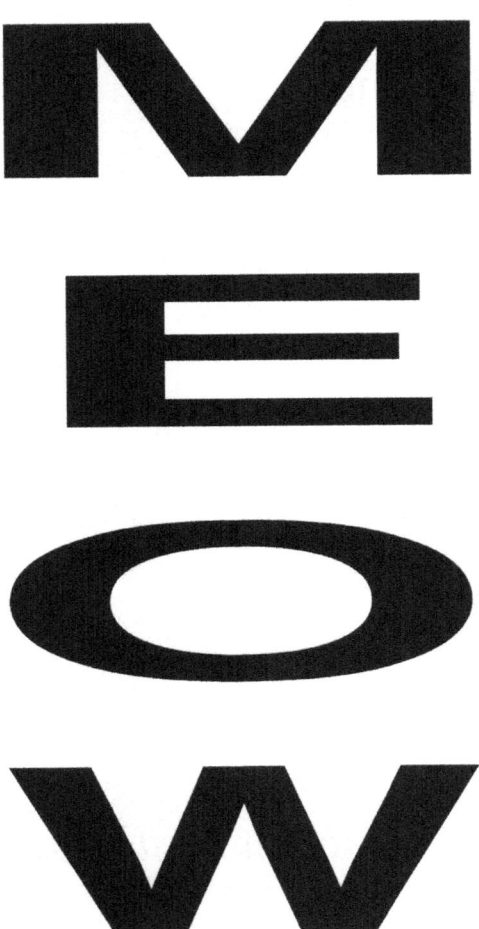

My cat is so fat, she makes *Godzilla* look like an action figure.

My cat is so fat, he was floating in the ocean and Spain claimed him for their new world.

My cat is so fat that when she goes outside, we go into daylight savings time.

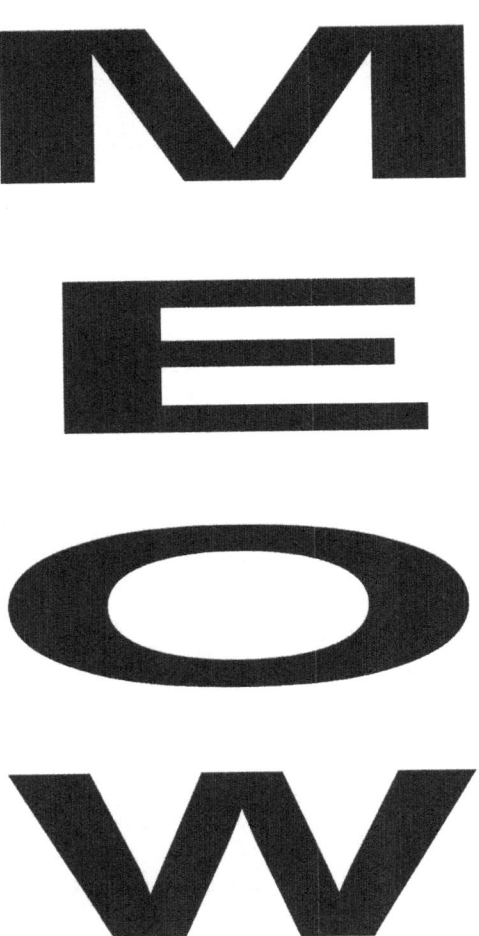

My cat is so fat that he needs to wear a tracker on both front and back paws because of time zone difference.

My cat is so fat a water park hired her to sit in the pool and start flapping her thighs together to make waves.

Why did the fat cat get stuck in the doggie door? Because it was a little husky.

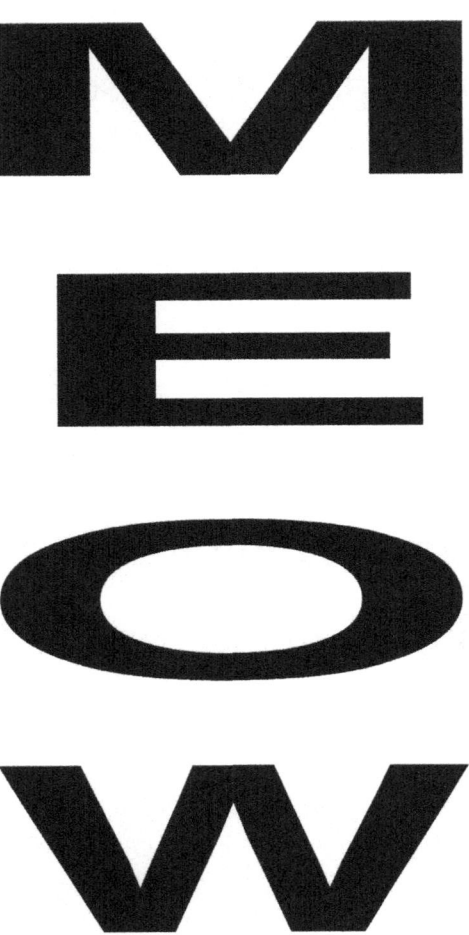

My cat is so fat, it wasn't the stork that brought him. It was a monster crane! *(Yeah, a metal one)*

My cat is so fat... I know six fat cats, and she's 5 of them.

What's the difference between a compulsive cat and a fat cat? One has OCD and the other has OBCD.

My cat is so fat he ate my laptop because the website said it had cookies in it.

My cat is so fat and old that she's still eating from the *last supper.*

My cat is so fat that when we cook his dinner we use a *Macro*-wave instead of micro-wave.

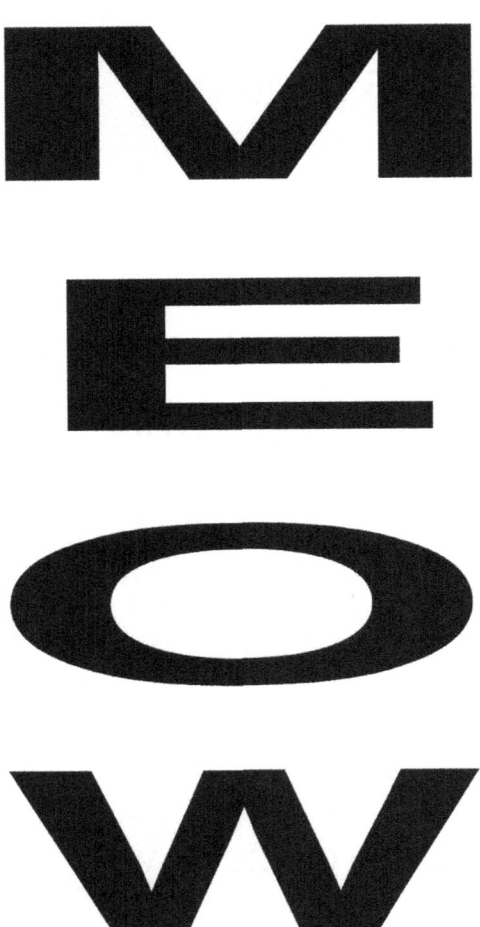

My cat is so fat her blood type
is A ... (& W).

My cat is so fat I swerved to
miss him and my car ran outta
gas!!

My cat is so fat she took a bath
in the lake and it flooded three
near by cities.

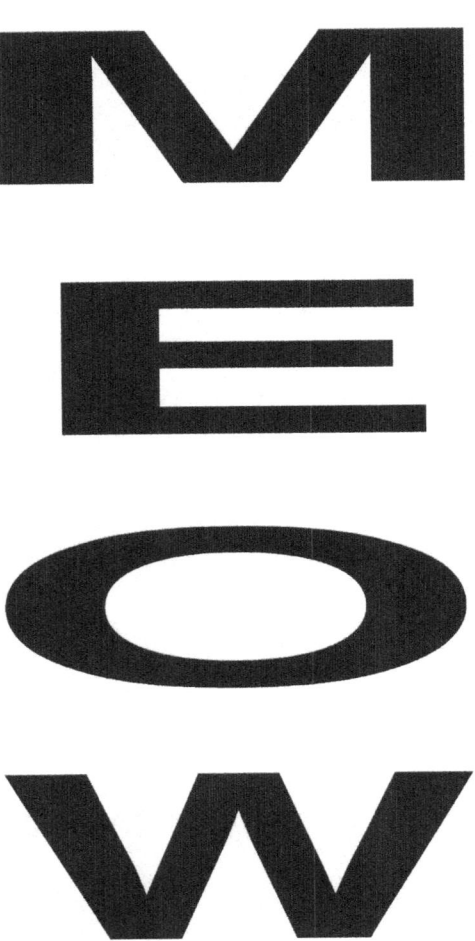

My cat is so fat when he goes to the beach, *Greenpeace* shows up to try and drag him back into the ocean.

My cat is so fat and so old that she's currently rolling over in her gravy.

We shouldn't make any jokes about fat cats. They've got enough on their plate already.

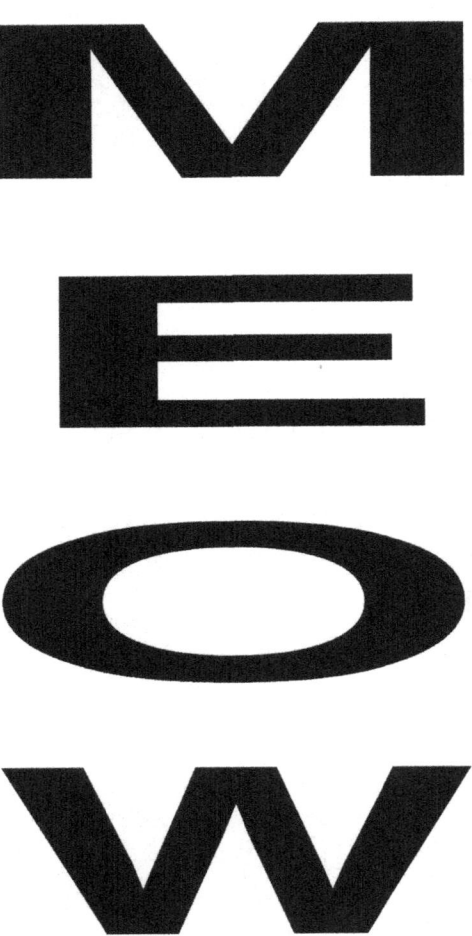

My cat is so fat when he runs acrosss the street he leaves potholes.

My cat is so fat when she fell...
I didn't laugh, but the ground cracked up.

My cat is so fat when he stepped on the scale, it said, *one at a time, please.*

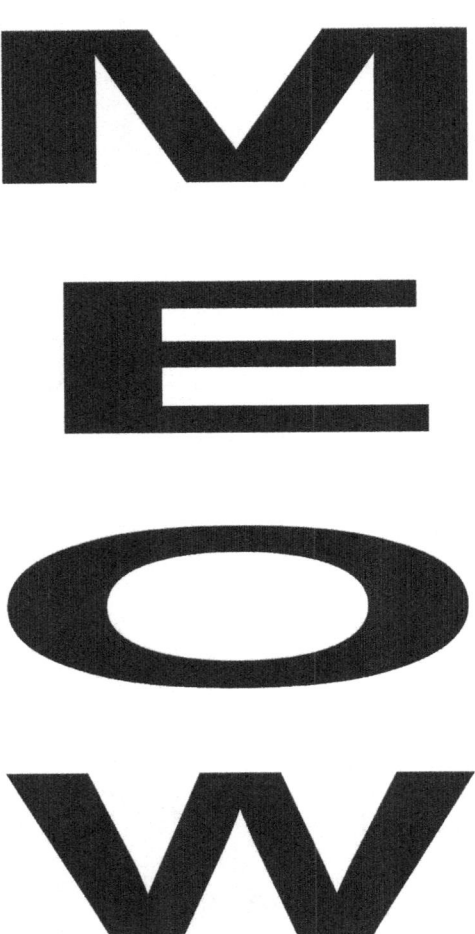

My cat is so fat that by the time she passed by the TV, all the World Series games had been played.

My cat is so fat he comes with his own gravity field.

My cat is so fat that it takes 2 bus transfers, and a train ride to find her good side.

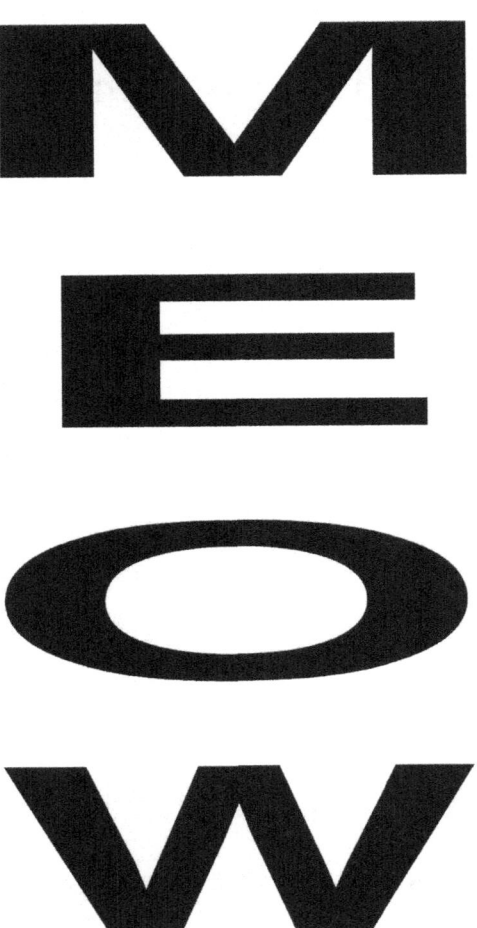

My cat is so fat that when I entered his weight into my fitness app, it said "Please enter your weight, not your social security number."

My cat is so fat that when she was invited to the Super Bowl, she asked if *spoons* were included.

My cat is so fat... *(Add your own cat fat joke here)*.

What do you call a cat who ate too many sweets? A fat cat-astrophe.

My cat is so that when she took a Christmas picture, it took until Valentine's day to finish printing.

My cat's body is so fat that on sunny days we can rent him out as *shade*.

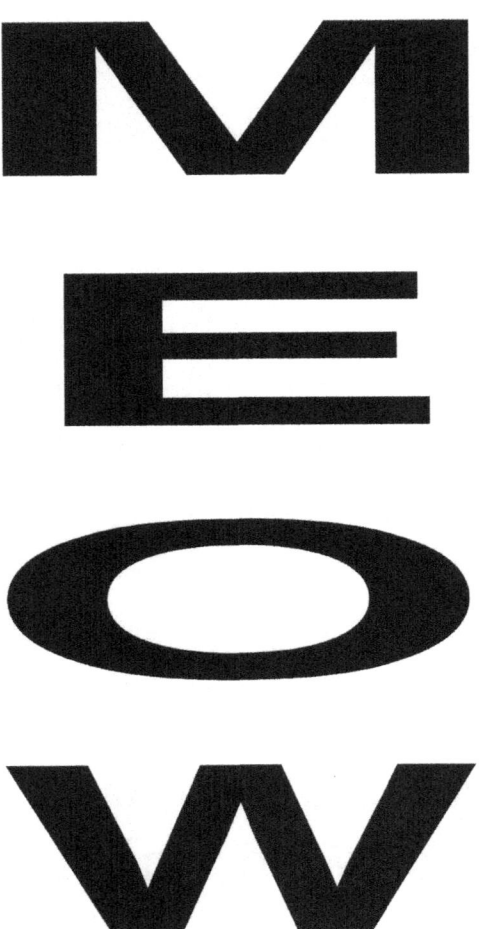

The best benefit of my cat being fat is that she is least likely to be stolen.

My cat no longer enjoys amusement parks because kids keep asking to ride him.

My cat jumped into the swimming pool and the kids jumped out shouting, *"Tsuna*

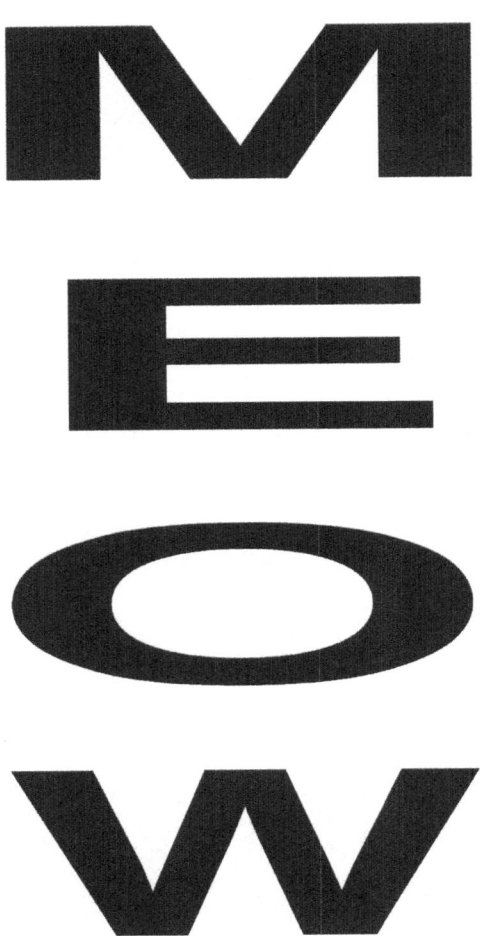

My cat is so fat that we get a group insurance discount to insure just her.

My cat is so fat that flesh eating bacteria die from exhaustion.

My cat is so fat that I recovered 2 TB of storage on my phone when I deleted a picture of him.

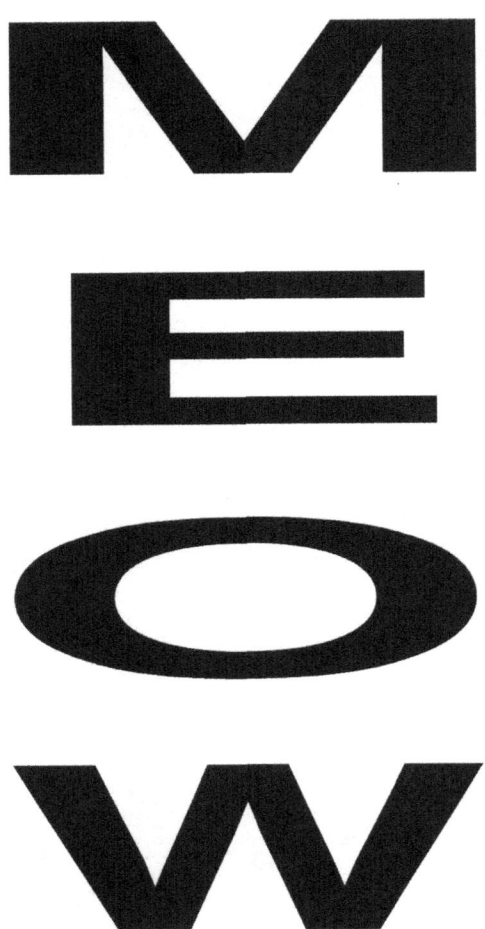

My cat is so fat that when we visit the zoo, the people feed her peanuts.

My cat is so fat that I wasn't kidding when I said the world revolves around him.

What can you do to help a fat cat lose weight? Tie a cupcake to a moving car's bumper.

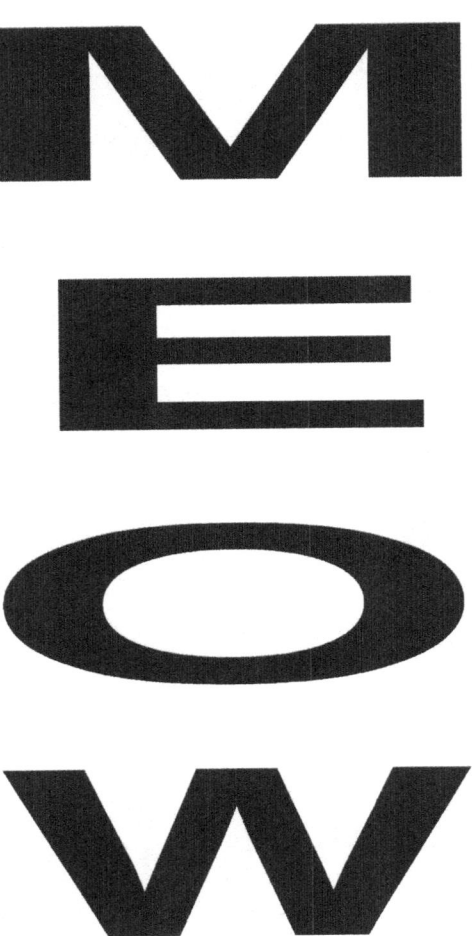

My cat plays Hide and Seek with losing weight, but it always finds her.

My cat is so fat it has more rolls than a bakery.

If your fat cat weighs 44 pounds on the Earth, but only 12 pounds on the Mars, it means they're not fat, but just living on the wrong planet.

MEOW

A girl takes her big fat cat to the vet.

"My cat is very fat," she says.

"Alright," says the vet. "I will look at him."

The vet picks up the cat and examines its teeth. Then she looks at its eyes. Then into its ears. Finally, she turns to the girl and says, "I'm very sorry. I'm going to have to put your cat down."

"Oh no! Because he's so fat?"

"Yes," says the doctor. "My arms are killing me."

How do fat cats hide from exercise? By joining a *fitness protection* program.

How do you burn calories fastest? Set a fat cat on fire.

What do fat cats do when they get depressed? They cut themselves... a piece of *cake*.

What is the best way to look thin and slim? By hanging out with fat cats.

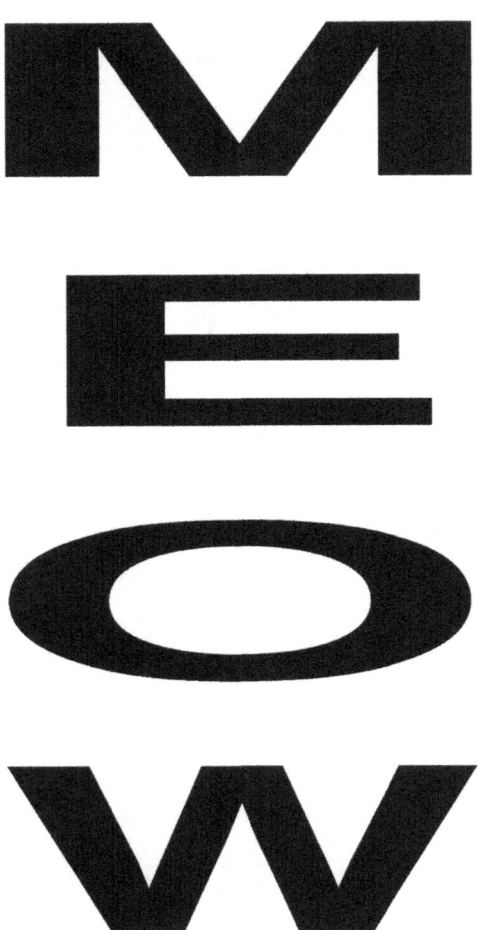

Which movement is the only movement without movement? *Fat Acceptance.*

Why do fat cats think obesity is not a problem? Since heat makes things expand, they think they are just hot.

What is a popular funny saying among fat cats? *Once you go fat, you never go back.*

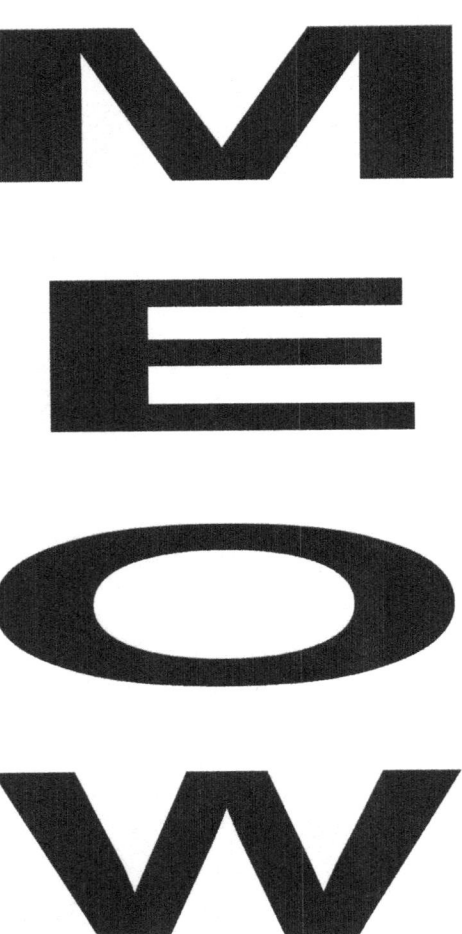

Why do you think obesity does not run in a fat cat's family? Well, actually no one runs in a fat cat's family.

My cat is so fat when she stepped on the scale it said, "To be continued."

My cat is so fat, when he went bungee jumping, he broke the *bridge!*

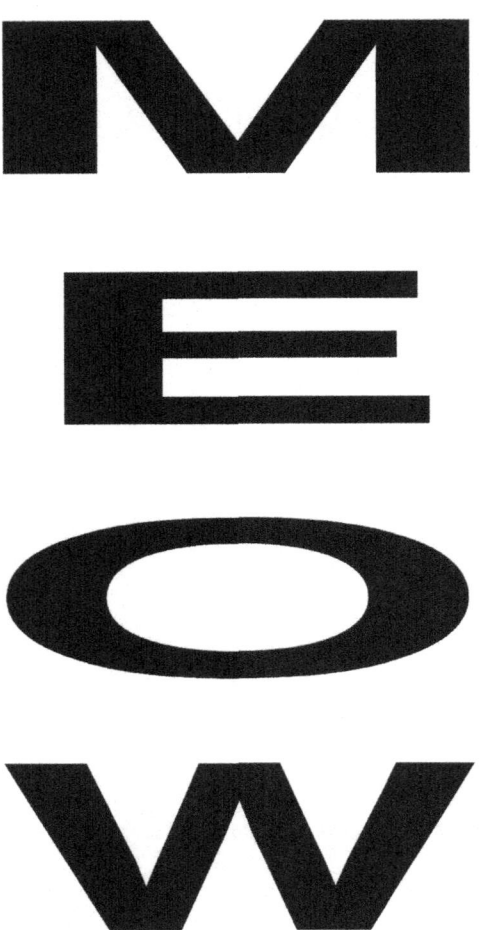

My cat is so fat when we applied for the *Biggest Loser* TV show for animals, they said, "Sorry, there's a weight limit."

I told my cat that the only way to look thinner was to hang out with really fat cats.

My fat cat wanted to lose 10 pounds this year. Only 13 to go.

My cat is so fat, she fell down and rocked herself to sleep trying to get up!

My cat is so fat that the only way I can fit his whole body into a photo is to use *panorama*.

Fat cats are lucky - they get to eat whatever they want and not worry about getting fat.

I'm hungry. Let's eat…

MEOW

About the Joke Stealer *(Rather, Author)*

Nick Hetcher is the self-proclaimed "Godfather of Cat Jokes." He's the long-time husband to Lynn (who has had to put up with his "jokes" for far too long), he's a dad to 4 great kids (Melissa, Nicolas, Destiny, and Ginny). He's also a granddad (papa) to 15 super kids (Ashley, Brandon, Rosa, Lexie, Clayton, Kayden, Gavin, Carsten, Sienna, Sawyer, Silas, Ollie, Zac, Izzy, Gracelynn, and great granddad to 2 more awesome kids (Anna and Aubrey). They don't always love his jokes, but do love the candy bribes for laughing at them.

*Please giv*e me a good review on Amazon.

CatJokeBook.com

Other Joke Books by Nick Hetcher

THE "COFFEE" JOKE BOOK
TheCoffeeJokeBook.com

THE ENCYCLOPEDIA OF DAD JOKES DadJokeBook.com

Made in the USA
Monee, IL
25 July 2023

39858897R00059